Coloring Tips & Tricks

Volume 1

The Coloring Handbook

Coloring Pages

Coloring Techniques & Step by Step Tutorials

Easy to follow Step by Step Tutorials

Lesson Worksheets

Inspirational Projects

written & illustrated by Anne Manera

Use Any Brand of Coloring Medium

The Coloring Handbook
Volume 1
Coloring Techniques & Step by Step Tutorials
by Anne Manera

Improve your coloring skills with this easy to use coloring handbook. This book is a reference guide for coloring hobby enthusiasts of all skill levels. This book includes coloring techniques, step by step coloring tutorials and information for your coloring hobby, that can easily be applied to any coloring book page or creative art project. Any brand of any mediums used in this book can be used to achieve similar results. Information on various techniques & step by step tutorials are included along with coloring pages for you to practice what you have learned.

Topics

Blending & Shading with Colored Pencils
Grayscale Illustration
Pointillism
Monochromatic
Just a #2 pencil
Oil Pastels
Gel Crayons
Impressionism
Stained Glass Effect
Chalk Pastels
Create Texture with Tape
Adding Doodles
Blending Solvents
3D Coloring Pages
Gel Pens
Wood Grain Effect
Color Theory
Glossary of Terms
Resources for Art Supplies
Coloring Pages
Techniques Practice Worksheets

About the Author

The author and artist, Anne Manera, illustrates coloring books for adults and kids, and also hosts online coloring tutorial videos that demonstrate a variety of coloring techniques. Anne Manera's coloring books are available on multiple topics including simple designs, complicated designs, animal themed and whimsical illustrations including skills from beginner to advanced levels. She holds a Bachelor of Art and Master of Art, with a concentration on graphic design and media arts. Anne has illustrated and self-published over 200 books, on topics including coloring, cooking, journaling, kids books, and coloring tutorials. She is best known in the coloring community and social media platforms for her coloring video tutorials and COLOR-ALONGs which she presents on a regular basis.

Follow Anne Manera

Website -
www.annemanera.com

Amazon Author Page -
www.amazon.com/author/annemanera

Facebook -
www.facebook.com/annemanerascoloringbooks

YouTube -
www.youtube.com/annemaneracoloringbooks

Instagram -
www.instagram.com/anne.manera

Pinterest -
www.pinterest.com/manera

Email -
designer@annemanera.com

Join Email List -
www.annemanera.com

Podcast -
www.annemanera.com

Copyright © 2019 Anne Manera
All rights reserved. No part of this publication may be reproduced, stored in a retrieval system, or transmitted, in any form or by any means, electronic, mechanical, photocopying, recording or otherwise, without prior written permission from the author.

Photographs sourced from Pixabay
ISBN-13: 9781074835699

Your Coloring Hobby

Tips & Tricks

Keep Your Pencils Sharpened

Color Topics You Enjoy

Relax Your Hands

Take Your Time

Never Compare Yourself to Others

Benefits of Coloring

Sparks Creativity

Helps you Relax

It's Fun & Simple

Reduces Stress

Stimulates the Brain

Relieves Anxiety

Distracts Your Mind

Enhances Motor Skills

Photographing Your Pages

Lay the Page Flat on a Table

Turn off overhead lighting

Hold camera directly above the page

Use the light on your camera

Photograph outdoors if possible

Get Social

Join a Facebook Coloring Group

Join a Local In Person Coloring Group

Share your finished pages on social media

Table of Contents

The Color Wheel	7
Coloring Supplies	8
Blending Solvents	9
Step by Step Tutorial Gel Crayons Layering Colors	10
Step by Step Tutorial Gel Pens Mandala	12
Adding Doodles	14
Bolding	16
Coloring Pages in 3D	18
Stained Glass	20
Creating Texture with Tape	22
Step by Step Tutorial Wood Grain Effect Mandala	24
Step by Step Tutorial with Cray Pas Oil Pastels	26
Step by Step Tutorial Grayscale Illustration	28
Colored Pencils Blending	30
Colored Pencils Shading	32
Pointillism	34
Chalk Pastels	36
Impressionism	38
Monochromatic	40
Just a #2 Pencil	42
Glossary	44
Resources	45
Notes	46
Coloring Pages	51-97

**Download FREE Extra Worksheets
at www.annemanera.com/coloringhandbook
with code HANDBOOK**

The Color Wheel

A Color Wheel is a great reference tool for coloring. Each time multiple colors are used, a new color scheme is created. Experiment with different colors to learn how colors relate to one another and to get a better understanding of what colors appeal to you.

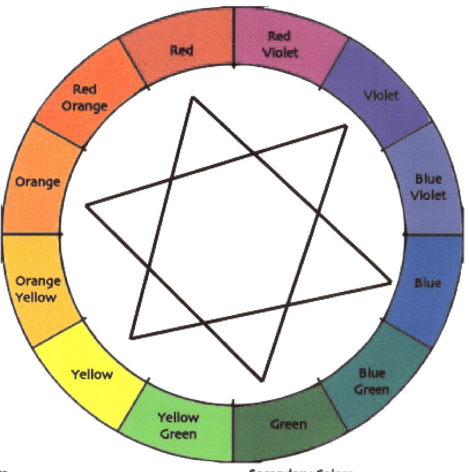

Primary Colors –
can be mixed together to make any color

Secondary Colors –
created by mixing primary colors

Complementary Colors – opposites on the color wheel & look good together

Coloring Supplies

Colored Pencils - available as wax based, oil based or woodless. Each type has a colored lead at its core. Colored pencils can be blended together or with a blending solvent.

Gel Pens - this pen is very popular with many adults who color. A gel pen is just like a regular pen but the ink flows much easier and they are available in glitter, metallic and basic colors.

Markers - there are so many types of markers - water based, alcohol based, permanent, fine tips, chiseled tip, wide tip, felt tip, non toxic - each type is a personal choice.

Oil Pastels - similar to a soft wax crayon, these pastels can be blended together, blended with a blending solvent and can be used to create a variety of textures.

Gel Crayons - this type of crayon looks like a tube of lipstick and can be blended together and used with water to create a watercolor effect.

#2 Pencils - a basic pencil, also referred to as a graphite pencil, can be used to color either an entire page or just an area of a page. This pencil can also be used to unclog an electric pencil sharpener simply by sharpening this pencil when their is a jam.

Chalk Pastels - available as pencils or in sticks. Chalk pastel pencils can be sharpened just like a pencil, but be sure to use a handheld sharpener for these pencils as they tend to break off inside an electric pencil sharpener. Chalk pastel sticks are in a rectangle shape and are great for creating backgrounds or coloring larger areas.

Crayons - amazing results can be achieved with a basic crayon which is often thought of as only being suitable for coloring by kids. However, the crayon can be blended with blending solvents and can be used just like a colored pencil for blending & shading.

Blending Solvent - this is used to blend a variety of mediums to create a very smooth to a color. Using a blending solvent is optional.

Pencil Sharpeners - there are two types of pencil sharpeners available - handheld and electric or battery operated. The handheld version can be a bit clumsy to use and does not produce as sharp a point on a pencil as an electric or battery operated sharpener.

Blending Solvents

Blending Solvents are products used to blend colored pencils, crayons, oil pastels, gel crayons, gel pens, markers and many other coloring mediums. The purpose of using a blending solvent is to create a smooth appearance to an area that has been colored. Using a blending solvent is not necessary and is up to the individual person when deciding to use one.

Types of Blending Solvents

Rubbing Alcohol - this works great with colored pencils as the alcohol breaks down the wax residue left from the colored pencil.

Petrolueum Jelly - this works great with colored pencils as the petroleum jelly blends the lead from the colored pencils to create a smooth less grainy appearance.

Baby Oil or Mineral Oil - this type of oil works well for creating a very saturated color. The oil blends well with colored pencils, crayons or gel crayons.

Cooking Oil - any type of cooking oil - canola, vegetable, corn, olive, coconut - all work well for blending colored pencils and crayons. Cooking oil works in the same way as baby oil or mineral oil.

Gamsol - this product can be found in art supply stores and is an odorless mineral spirits base. Works well for blending colored pencils, wax or oil based pencils.

Water - this works well for blending gel crayons, water based markers and some brands of gel pens.

Products Used to Blend Solvents

Cotton Swabs
Tissues
Paper Towels
Cotton Balls
Paint brush
Make up Sponge

- Apply your blending solvent to your coloring page after it has been colored when using colored pencils or crayons.
- Oils and petroleum jelly will take time to dry. Be patient.
- Use rubbing alcohol in a well ventilated room.
- Water used for gel crayons & markers can be used as you are coloring. Be mindful of placing your hand on wet areas.
- Don't use too much of any blending solvent. It's easy to add more, but messy to remove too much.

Step by Step Coloring Tutorial
Gel Crayons Layering Colors

In this tutorial Gel Pens are layered to create a textured background behind the angel. Any brand of Gel Crayons can be used for this tutorial. Colors needed are blue, green & dark blue. Use short strokes when coloring with Gel Crayons to create a textured appearance. Colors can be blended to create a new color by using colors atop of one another.

Begin with a medium blue color in Images #1 & #2 applying short strokes to create a textured appearance behind the angel. Continue to fill the background as shown in image #3. Add green to the background as shown in image #4. Continue to use short strokes on top of the blue background. Begin to fill in the white spaces amidst the blue background with green.

Fill the entire background with green atop of the blue as shown in image #5. Add a darker blue atop of the medium blue and green as shown in images #7 & #8. Keep applying short strokes to the white spaces between the colors until the entire background is filled in with color.

The page used in this tutorial can also be found in Simple Little Angels Coloring Book for Adults by Anne Manera

Gel Crayons Worksheet

Using the boxes below, practice short strokes & blending with gel crayons as you combine 2 or more colors atop of one another or by creating a gradual transition from one color to the next.

Yellow + Blue

Yellow + Red

Red + Blue + Yellow

Use the boxes below to practice more short strokes & blending with gel crayons

Step by Step Coloring Tutorial
Gel Pens Mandala

Any brand of Gel Pens can be used for this tutorial. Colors needed are blue, pink, purple, green & yellow. Use short strokes when coloring with Gel Pens to create a smooth base of color. Colors can be blended to create a new color by using colors atop of one another. Apply a heavy pressure to create a darker color.

As you apply colors to this mandala with Gel Pens, remember to use short strokes and heavy pressure to obtain a solid color. In image #1 & #2 pink, yellow & purple are added to different sections of the mandala. In image #3 & #4 blue is added next to the pink. Heavy pressure is applied using the pink to obtain a deep pink color.

  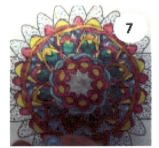 

Continue on to the next section of the mandala with yellow as shown in image #5. Image #6 continues with pink towards the outer section of the mandala. In images #7 & #8, other areas of the mandala have been filled in with the green and yellow in various sections. Placement of color is up to each individual. Allow yourself to relax as you color paying attention to creating short strokes with the Gel Pens.

The page used in this tutorial can also be found in Comforting Mandalas Grief Healing Coloring Book by Anne Manera

Gel Pens Worksheet

Using the boxes below, practice short strokes with gel pens as you combine 2 or more colors atop of one another or by creating a gradual transition from one color to the next.

Yellow + Blue

Yellow + Red

Red + Blue + Yellow

Use the boxes below to practice more short strokes & blending with gel pens

Adding Doodles

Adding doodles to your coloring page allows you to enhance your coloring page with lines, shapes, patterns and more. Drawing skills are not needed to fill areas of a coloring page with your own designs. Plus, there are so many benefits to letting your mind wander and creating different types of shapes and patterns.

Practice the patterns below by drawing the lines & shapes you see in the boxes to the left in the boxes to the right. Use a pencil, pen or gel pen.

Benefits of Doodling

Concentration - elevates focus allowing you to concentrate with ease

Problem Solving - allows you to figure out new ways to solve a problem

The Big Picture - encourages you to be aware of how to develop a strategy

Exploration - doodling improves the brain's ability to find new ways of of doing everyday tasks

Think Beyond - encourages you to think beyond normal everyday routines

Creativity - exercises your imagination

Memory - enable you to remember more important information

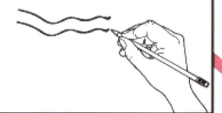

Doodling Worksheet

Using the boxes below, create patterns, lines and shapes for more doodling practice. Keep as a reference to for coloring pages. Use any medium of your choice - pens, pencils, markers, colored pencils, gel pens, crayon.

Bolding

Bolding is a basic technique that most people have used since childhood. Bolding simply involves tracing over the black lines of an illustration with a marker, crayon, colored pencil or gel pen so that the line becomes thicker. When applying this technique, the area of an illustration is outlined, creating an emphasis on that area. The area inside the lines is then colored with a lighter color. It can be the same shade of the outline color or a different color completely. Bolding is a great technique to practice using the color wheel to become familiar with primary colors, complementary colors and color schemes.

In the examples below, each flower is outlined with marker and then filled in with crayon or colored pencil. The purple flower has been bolded with a purple marker and a purple crayon. The pink flower has been bolded with a pink marker and colored with a pink colored pencil. Any brand marker, crayon or colored pencil can be used for bolding.

The page used in this tutorial can also be found in Peaceful Evening Variety Coloring Book by Anne Manera

Coloring Pages in 3D

In January 2019, 3Dimensional Coloring Pages became a hot new coloring craze! The 3D effect creates the illusion that parts of the illustration has depth and parts of the illustration are hovering atop of one another. Coloring pages with this 3D effect produce stunning results with little effort or skill level. The gray areas of the illustration allow it to appear to be shaded. Colored pencils or crayons are best for coloring 3D coloring pages so the gray areas will still be visible. However, gel pens and alcohol markers work great too! 3D pages can also be colored with digitally with coloring apps.

Gel Pens   Colored Pencils   Digital app

Practice coloring 3D illustrations with these simple 3D illustrations below.

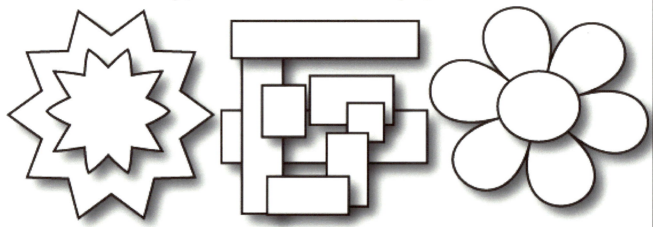

The pages referenced on this page can be found in
Mandalas in 3D Coloring Book Volumes 1 & 2 and 3D Variety Coloring Book by Anne Manera

3D Coloring Worksheet

Practice 3D Coloring with different mediums - colored pencils, markers or crayons.

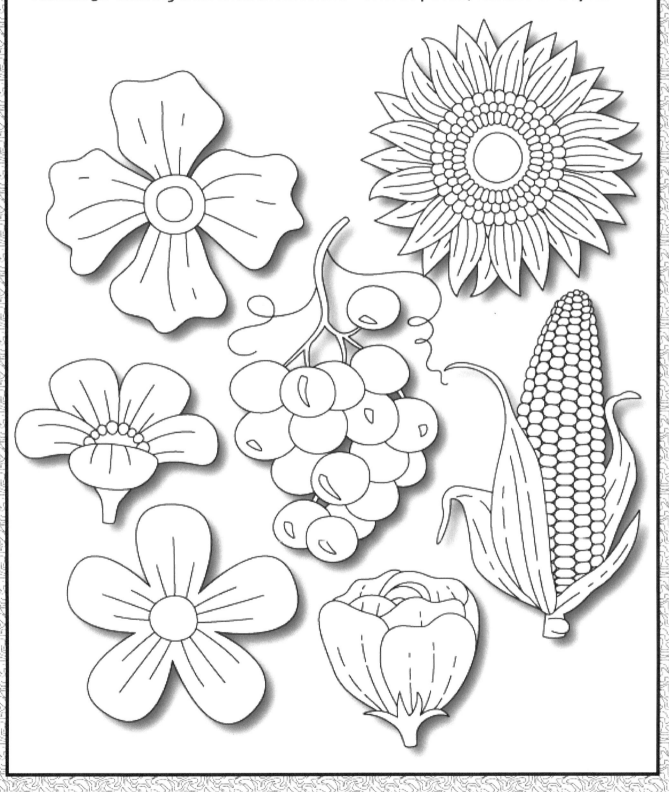

Stained Glass

Create a Stained Glass effect on any coloring page by simply coloring with any brand of crayons and then applying a blending oil on top of the colored areas. Blending oils can be any type of oil such as olive oil, coconut oil, canola, vegetable, corn, baby oil, mineral oil. The oil can be applied with a paintbrush or cotton swab.

First Row – Begin coloring the entire coloring page with a light color. This will create a base coat of color that will be behind your final colors and will help to create a glow behind the page. In this example, a yellow crayon is used to color the base coat of color.

Second Row – Once the base coat of color is applied, the top final colors can be added just as you would color any page with crayons.

Third Row – In this last step begin to add your blending oil on top of the colors. The oil will begin to blend the color and create a semi transparent look to your coloring page, giving the appearance of stained glass.

The page used in this tutorial can also be found in Bursting Mandalas An Easy on the Eyes Coloring Book by Anne Manera

Stained Glass Worksheet

Practice blending crayons with a blending oil in the boxes below.

Creating Texture with Tape

Adding texture to a coloring page can often times enhance the finished page. Colors can be enhanced, altered or muted, simply by placing something behind your coloring page and coloring on top of it. In this tutorial masking tape is used to create a texture on the vases. Other items that can be placed behind a coloring page to create texture include - string, plastic wrap, crumpled paper, crumpled aluminum foil, slotted spatulas, leaves. The possibilities are unlimited and most items can be found in your own home.

Attach masking tapes pieces varying in sizes between 1/2 inch to 1 inch onto a piece of paper forming a sort of tape collage. Place your coloring page on top of the tape collage and begin to color with a colored pencil. Hold your pencil at a slight angle so you are coloring with the side of the lead of the pencil.

Vary the pressure you are using as you color on top of the tape. Notice the lines that are created by the edges of the tape. You can use any type of tape - masking, scotch, duct, wasabi. New textures can be created with different types of tape.

The page used in this tutorial can also be found in Tiny Crowds Coloring Book for All by Anne Manera

Textures with Tape Worksheet

Using the boxes below, place different types of tape on a table and color over it with crayons, oil pastels, colored pencils or markers. Notice how different types of tape create different textures.

Color with 3 Shades of Blue

Color with 3 Shades of Purple

Color with 3 Shades of Green

Color with Orange & Yellow

Color with Blue, Gray & Brown

Color with Red & Yellow

Color with Green, Yellow & Blue

Color with Red, Orange & Blue

Use the boxes below to practice more textures with various tapes and mediums

Step by Step Coloring Tutorial
Wood Grain Effect Mandala

Any brand of colored pencil can be used for this tutorial. Colors needed are light brown, medium brown, dark brown & black. Pay attention to the varying degrees of pressure applied to each area as you create various shades of browns and blacks. To achieve the wood grain effect, color lightly throughout the page, leaving the graininess to show through.

Use light brown with light to medium pressure to color the center.

Color over the light brown with a darker brown.

Using a reddish brown color the petals shading from dark to light.

Continue with dark to light shading on all petals.

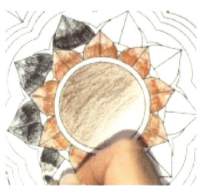

Using black color the next layer of petals with dark to light shading.

Using dark brown color in between the petals with a heavy pressure.

Use a medium brown for the outer circle coloring from light to dark.

Lightly color the next outer circle with light black.

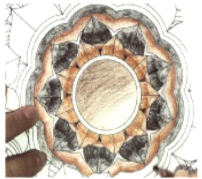

Finish up with light black for the outer circle.

The page used in this tutorial can also be found in Tangled Mandalas A Complicated Coloring Book by Anne Manera

Wood Grain Effect Worksheet

Using the boxes below, practice coloring with varying degrees of pressure with colored pencils, blending different shades of browns.

Step by Step Coloring Tutorial with Cray Pas Oil Pastels

The brand used in this tutorial is presented as an example. Any brand of oil pastel can be used for this tutorial by simply using similar colors.

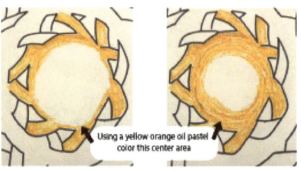

Using a yellow orange oil pastel color this center area

Using a yellow oil pastel color on top of the previous color

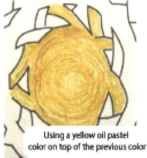

Add an orange oil pastel on top of the previous colors. Blend colors with a cotton swab or your fingers

Color this area with a bright yellow oil pastel

Add green oil pastel on top of the yellow and blend together

Using bright red oil pastel color these areas with heavy pressure

Add bright blue oil pastel to the areas pictured here

Using your fingers or a cotton swab blend your colors in each area

The page used in this tutorial can also be found in Tribal Abstract Coloring Book for All by Anne Manera

Oil Pastels Worksheet

Using the boxes below, practice blending different colors with oil pastels.

Step by Step Coloring Tutorial
Grayscale Illustration

The brand used in this tutorial is presented as an example. Any brand of colored pencil can be used for this tutorial by simply using similar colors.

Crayola Pencil Colors Used
Pink, Mahogany, Blue, Golden Yellow, Orange, Violet, White

Using a pink pencil color the entire pitcher with a light pressure

Using a Maghogany pencil color over the pink with a light pressure

Using a Blue pencil color the entire bowl with a light pressure

Using a Blue pencil color the entire bowl with a light pressure atop of your first layer of Blue

Using a Golden Yellow pencil color the entire backrgound with a light pressure

Using an Orange pencil color the entire background atop of the first layer of Golden Yellow

Using a Purple pencil color the entire table with a light pressure

Using a White pencil color the lightest areas of each object with a light pressure

The page used in this tutorial can also be found in Still Life Grayscale Illustration Coloring Book by Anne Manera

Grayscale Illustration Worksheet

Practice with a coloring grayscale illustrations with colored pencils. Pay close attention to the shading in these illustrations as you apply colors.

Colored Pencils Blending

Image A

Blending with colored pencils involves mixing of 2 or more colors to create a new color or to create a new shade of the same color. It is important to remember to apply the same pressure as you apply each color so you will create a seamless transition. In the image to the left (A) notice how the vase on the right is blended with yellow and brown to create a rust color. Brown & yellow were used to color this vase.

Tip - don't hold your pencil too tight - Relax your hand

In the image to the right (B) each petal of the sunflower is blended with a hot pink color and a shade of yellow towards the outer section of each petal. The transition between the 2 colors is seamless as it creates a new color in the middle section of the petal.

Image B

Image C

In the image above (C) 2 colors, blue & yellow are blended together, creating green in the middle as the 2 colors overlap. The image (D) below includes a blend of 3 colors - blue, yellow & red. As each color is blended, new colors are created. Blue blends to yellow to create green and yellow blends to red to create orange.

Experiment with blending different colors and different brands of colored pencils to for different results. The possibilities are endless.

Image D

The pages used in this tutorial can also be found in The Still Life Coloring Book Coloring Book by Anne Manera and Anne Manera's Coloring Camp Spring 2019 Book by Anne Manera

Colored Pencils Blending Worksheet

Using the boxes below, practice blending with colored pencils as you combine 2 or more colors atop of one another or by creating a gradual transition from one color to the next.

Yellow + Blue

Yellow + Red

Red+ Blue

Use the boxes below to practice more Blending with colored pencils

Colored Pencils Shading

Learning to shade with colored pencils is a technique that can be applied to many other coloring mediums such as oil pastels, chalk pastels, alcohol markers, #2 pencil and gel pens. Applying varying degrees of pressure with colored pencils will result in a variety of shades of one color or many colors.

In the image to the right (A) notice how the blue towards the center of the flower is darker than the outer portion of the petals. Heavier pressure was applied towards the center and the pressure became lighter towards the edge of the flower's petal.

Image A

Image B

In the image above (B) many layers of color was applied to achieve shading on the pumpkins & the blades of grass.

Key Points to Remember when Shading with Colored Pencils

1. Pressure -
Simply adjusting how much pressure you apply to you coloring page with your pencil, will alter the shade of color.

2. Less is more -
Begin your darker areas with a light pressure if you are unsure about how much pressure to apply. You can layer more color atop of one another to achieve a darker shade.

3. Sharp pencils -
Keep your pencils sharpened for best results.

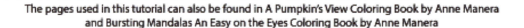

The pages used in this tutorial can also be found in A Pumpkin's View Coloring Book by Anne Manera and Bursting Mandalas An Easy on the Eyes Coloring Book by Anne Manera

Colored Pencils Shading Worksheet

Using the boxes below, practice shading with colored pencils using varying degrees of pressure. As you color from light to medium to heavy pressure, gradually apply more pressure to achieve a darker shading effect.

Light to Medium Pressure

Medium to Heavy Pressure

Light to Medium to Heavy Pressure

Use the boxes below to practice more Shading with colored pencils

Pointillism

Pointillism was developed by Georges Seurat and Paul Signac two Impressionist Artists most known for their paintings. Impressionist paintings are best viewed from a distance of approximately 5 feet and the same rule can be applied to Pointillism paintings. The further away the viewer stands from the painting, the less blurry the colors will appear.

The Pointillism technique can also be applied to coloring pages using a variety of mediums. Markers, gel pens and colored pencils are all good choices. The proximity of the dots is important to consider as new colors can be created based on how close or how far apart the dots are placed relative to one another. As you step further away from your finished coloring page, you will be able to see the new color you have created based on just how close the dots are placed.

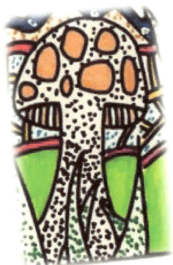

This same method of placement of the dots can be applied to create shading. The closer the dots are placed relative to one another, the darker the color will appear and the further apart the dots are placed relative to one another, the lighter the color will appear.

Keep in mind that not every area of the coloring page needs to be filled with dots. You can color areas of the page with a solid color and then apply dots atop the colored area to create a new color. For example, coloring an area with the color yellow and then applying blue dots will create the color

Learn more about Pointillism, Seurat & Signac

Pointillism - www.britannica.com/art/pointillism
Georges Seurat- www.georgesseurat.org
Paul Signac- hwww.paul-signac.org

The pages used in this tutorial can also be found in Funky Mandalas Coloring Book by Anne Manera, A Bug's View Coloring Book for All by Anne Manera and Butterfly Mandalas Coloring Book for Adults by Anne Manera

Pointillism Worksheet

The Pointillist Artists used dots to create colors and shading in a painting. When applying this same technique to a coloring page, using markers, gel pens and/or colored pencils, new colors are created based on the proximity of the dots. Using this worksheet, create new colors by placing dots next to one another in a variety of distances.

Make various shades of orange using yellow & red dots

- orange
- red-orange
- yellow-orange
- light orange

Make various shades of green using yellow & blue dots

- green
- yellow-green
- green-yellow
- light green

Make various shades of purple using blue & red dots

- purple
- red-purple
- blue-purple
- light purple

Use the boxes below to practice blending colors with dots.

35

Chalk Pastels

Chalk Pastels are available for coloring in two forms - sticks & pencils. Pastel sticks are typically rectangular in shape and when using them will result in chalk pastel on your hands. Pastel pencils are similar to colored pencils, but instead of lead encased in the wood, there is chalk pastel. Chalk Pastels can be used for the same techniques as colored pencils - blending, shading and burnishing.

Image A

Image B

Chalk pastels allow for opaque blending or a more transparent blending. In the image above (A), the areas colored in deep red have been blending once the color was applied to the page to create an opaque effect. In the image to the left (B), multiple colors are used to blend & shade. Blue is blended with yellow to create a green shade and red is blended with yellow to create an orange shade.

Applying a variety of pressure as you color with Chalk Pastels will create different shades of the same color.

A few things to keep in mind about Chalk Pastels-

-Chalk Pastels create dust, so use them in a well ventilated area
-Chalk Pastels will get your hands dirty
-A finished page can be sprayed with a fixative to seal the Chalk Pastels
-Chalk Pastels can be blending with your fingers, cotton swabs, tissue, a blending stump or paper towels
-Chalk Pastels are great for use on backgrounds
-Chalk Pastels are best sharpened in a non electric sharpener or with an xacto knife

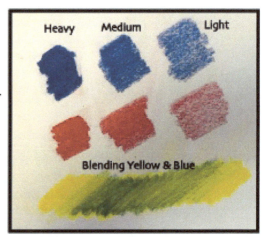

The pages used in this tutorial can also be found in Tribal Abstract Coloring Book by Anne Manera and Mandala Delight Coloring Book by Anne Manera

Chalk Pastels Worksheet

Using the boxes below, practice blending with chalk pastels as you combine 2 or more colors atop of one another or by creating a gradual transition from one color to the next.

Yellow + Blue

Yellow + Red

Red + Blue

Use the boxes below to practice more Blending with chalk pastels

Impressionism

Impressionism style of painting was developed in the late 1800's in Paris. Artists that painted in this style, used vivid colors and loose brushstrokes that often included short strokes that appeared choppy or blurry. Impressionistic paintings are best viewed from a distance of approximately 5-8 feet or when viewing closer, by squinting one's eyes. Linear perspective or proportion was not a focus of the Impressionistic Artist as they concentrated on the textures, movement and colors created by the brushstrokes. Subject matter included a variety ranging from landscapes to still lifes. Key dates 1867-1886.

When applying the Impressionism Style to coloring pages, a variety of mediums can be used - crayon, oil pastels, gel crayons, colored pencils, chalk pastels - to create the look of Impressionism. Focus on coloring with short strokes and vivid colors.

The first step is to color a base layer on the entire page in a light color. Then as you color each area of the illustration use short strokes with varying sizes and place them next to one another in varying places. Blending one, two or three shades of one color will create a texture. Blending multiple colors in one area will also create a texture and create rhythm.

You can learn more about Impressionist Artists -
Vincent Van Gogh, Claude Monet & Camille Pisarro
at the following websites -
Van Gogh - www.vangoghgallery.com
Monet - www.claude-monet.com
Pisarro - www.camille-pisarro.org

The page used in this tutorial can also be found in Lazy Waves Coloring Book for Adults by Anne Manera

Impressionism Worksheet

Using the boxes below, practice coloring in the Impressionist style with a variety of mediums. Color each box with light background color such as yellow or light orange. Next, using mulitiple color or multiple shades of the same color, color with short strokes to create the appearance of Impressionism.

Color with 3 Shades of Blue

Color with 3 Shades of Purple

Color with 3 Shades of Green

Color with Orange & Yellow

Color with Blue, Gray & Brown

Color with Red & Yellow

Color with Green, Yellow & Blue

Color with Red, Orange & Blue

Use the boxes below to practice more Impressionist style with various mediums

Monochromatic

Monochromatic colors are all the colors of a single shade of color. Each shade or tint of the same color when used together is considered a Monochromatic color scheme. The colors can be from a variety of mediums as long as they are in the same shades of a particular color.

When using a Monochromatic color scheme a few things need to be considered.

Shades - created when the base color is darkened with black

Advantages to using a Monochromatic color scheme on a coloring page -

Tones - created when the base color is mixed with gray

1. Create a visually cohesive look
2. Less stress when picking colors
3. Allows the colorist to focus on the coloring technique
4. Allow for a variety of mediums to be used

Tints - created when the base color is lightened with white

Black and white are not considered Monochromatic colors as they added to base colors to create different shades, tones and tints.

The pages referenced on this page can be found in
Graceful Mandalas Coloring Book & Journal and Cat Angels Coloring Book for All by Anne Manera

Monochromatic Worksheet

Monochromatic color shemes are created by using the same color in a variety of shades, tones and tints. Practice adding black, gray and white to the boxes below to achieve various shades, tones and tints

Shades

| base color | add black | more black | more black |

Tones

| base color | add gray | more gray | more gray |

Tints

| base color | add white | more white | more white |

Use the boxes below to practice more Monochromatic color schemes

Just a #2 Pencil

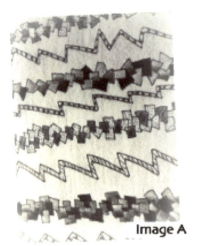
Image A

The #2 Pencil evokes memories of standardized testing in elementary school for many people. Filling in those little ovals so not a bit of white showed through in order for the test to be graded by a computer. The #2 Pencil is made from graphite, which is a natural element that is mined. Encased in wood, typically a shade of yellow, it's a pencil easily found in most people's homes and is very affordable. When a #2 Pencil is applied to coloring, the results can be amazing. So many different shades of gray can be achieved just by varying the pressure applied to the page with the pencil.

In the examples on this page, you can see the varying shades of gray created Just a #2 Pencil. In the image above (A) the background is a light shade of gray whilst the shapes are medium to dark grays. Each shade can be created by simply using a different pressure to the page. As you color with a #2 Pencil, it is also important to hold the pencil at a slight angle. This will allow for the graphite to be to applied the page evenly. In the image to the right (B), a speckled effect is created by creating dots on the page with the tip of the pencil. Shading from dark to light is achieved in the image below (C) by transitioning from a light to medium to heavy pressure.

Image B

Image C

Tips -
- Keep your pencil sharpened
- Hold your pencil at a slight angle
- Graphite will smudge when touched
- Different brand #2 pencils have different lead

The pages referenced on this page can be found in
Abstract Twist Coloring Book for All by Anne Manera, Simple Bird Mosaic Coloring Book for Adults by Anne Manera
and Easy Mandalas Coloring Book for All by Anne Manera

Just a #2 Pencil Worksheet

When you use a #2 Pencil, you can create a variety of shades of gray just by applying a different pressure. Use this worksheet to practice coloring with a #2 pencil to achieve a variety of shades. Be sure to keep the pencil at an angle as you color in order to have results that look smooth.

Light Pressure

Hold your pencil at a slight angle as you color with a light pressure.

Medium Pressure

Still keep your pencil at an angle but apply more pressure to the page.

Heavy Pressure

Still hold your pencil at an angle and apply a bit more pressure to the page

Use the boxes below to practice more shades of gray with a #2 pencil

Glossary

Burnishing - using many layers that you cannot see through

Opaque - cannot see through

Transparent - can see through

Highlight - the lightest spot of an area

Layering - use of color applied multiple times atop of one another

Light Source - the direction in which the light, natural or artificial is directed at an object

Lightfast - refers to how resistant a color is to fading when exposed to light

Blending - merging two or more colors to create a seamless transition

Shading - levels of darkness or lightness created by color

Primary Colors - red, yellow, blue which can be mixed to create secondary colors

Secondary Colors - purple, orange, green which can be created with primary colors

Rhythm - arrangement of visual elements allowing the viewers eye to move around

Composition - arrangement of visual elements

Symmetry - two sides are equal creating balance

Asymmetry - two sides are not identical or equal

Paper tooth - the surface or feel of the paper.

Mixed Media - use of many different art mediums in one page

Gradient - a smooth transition of one color into various shades of that same color

Balance - refers to the sense of distribution of colors, lines or shapes

Emphasis - an area of the coloring page given the most attention

Proportion - the relationship between two objects with respect to size

Contrast - arrangement of colors or shapes in relationship to one another

Hue - a color or shade that is true to a color

Saturation - intensity of the color

Tint - varying shades of one color

Value - lightness or darkness of colors

Blending Solvent - used to blend a coloring medium such as colored pencils

Resources

Amazrock- www.brands.amazrock.com

Arteza - www.arteza.com

Black Widow - www.blackwidowpencils.com

Crayola - www.crayola.com

Derwent - www.derwentart.com

Dick Blick - www.dickblick.com

Faber Castell - www.fabercastell.com

Gel Writer - www.ECR4kids.com

Jerry's Artarama - www.jerrysartarama.com

Maped- www.maped.com

Pentel - www.pentel.com

Prismacolor - www.prismacolor.com

Sakura- www.sakuraofamerica.com

Schpirerr Farben- www.schpirerrfarben.com

SMOOV - www.sosmoov.com

Staedtler - www.staedtler.us

Tombow - www.tombowusa.com

Notes

Notes

Coloring Pages

The following coloring pages are provided for you to practice the techniques and tutorials in this book.

Gel Crayons Coloring Page

Simple Little Angels Coloring Book for Adults by Anne Manera

The Coloring Handbook

Coloring Techniques & Step by Step Tutorials

written & illustrated by
Anne Manera

Gel Pens Coloring Page

Comforting Mandalas Grief Healing Coloring Book by Anne Manera

The Coloring Handbook

Coloring Techniques & Step by Step Tutorials

written & illustrated by
Anne Manera

Bolding Coloring Page

Peaceful Evening Variety Coloring Book by Anne Manera

The Coloring Handbook

Coloring Techniques & Step by Step Tutorials

written & illustrated by
Anne Manera

3D Coloring Page

Mandalas in 3D Coloring Book Volume 2 for All by Anne Manera

The Coloring Handbook

Coloring Techniques & Step by Step Tutorials

written & illustrated by
Anne Manera

Stained Glass Coloring Page

Bursting Mandalas An Easy on the Eyes Coloring Book by Anne Manera

The Coloring Handbook

Coloring Techniques & Step by Step Tutorials

written & illustrated by
Anne Manera

Textures Coloring Page

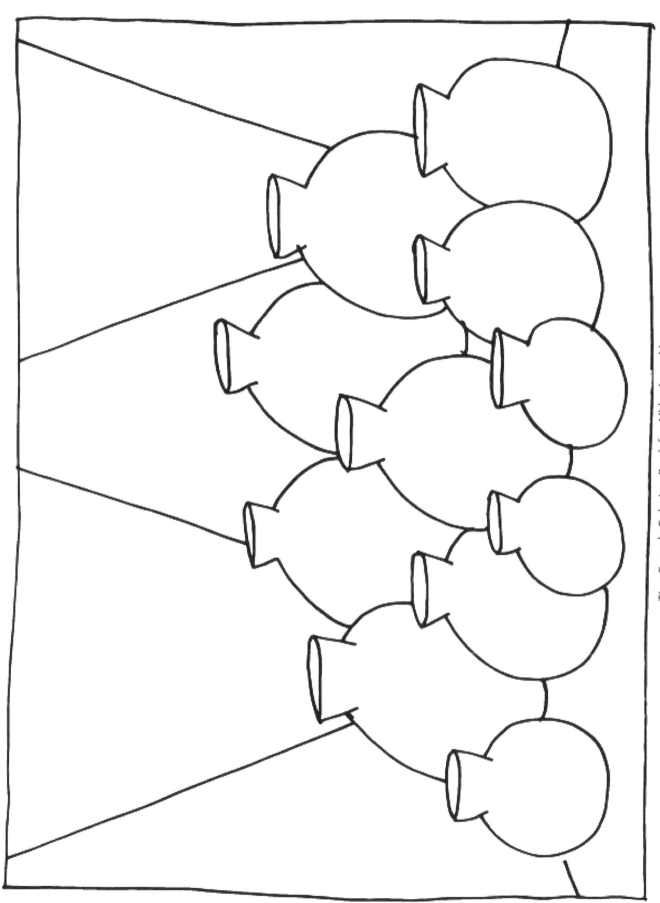

The Coloring Handbook

Coloring Techniques & Step by Step Tutorials

written & illustrated by
Anne Manera

Wood Grain Effect Coloring Page

Tangled Mandalas A Complicated Coloring Book by Anne Manera

The Coloring Handbook

Coloring Techniques & Step by Step Tutorials

written & illustrated by
Anne Manera

The Coloring Handbook

Coloring Techniques & Step by Step Tutorials

written & illustrated by
Anne Manera

Grayscale Illustration Coloring Page

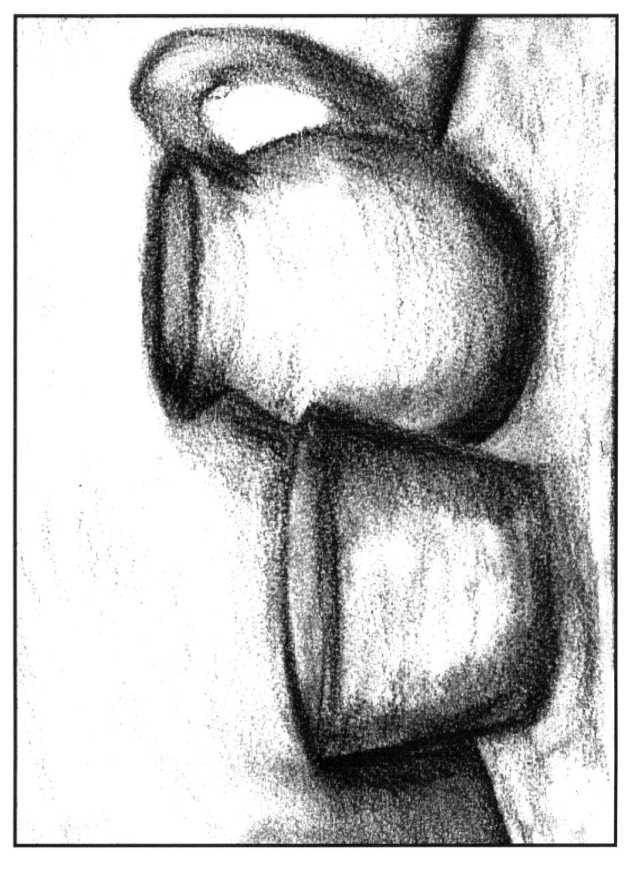

The Coloring Handbook

Coloring Techniques & Step by Step Tutorials

written & illustrated by
Anne Manera

Colored Pencils Blending Coloring Page

The Coloring Handbook

Coloring Techniques & Step by Step Tutorials

written & illustrated by
Anne Manera

Colored Pencils Blending Coloring Page

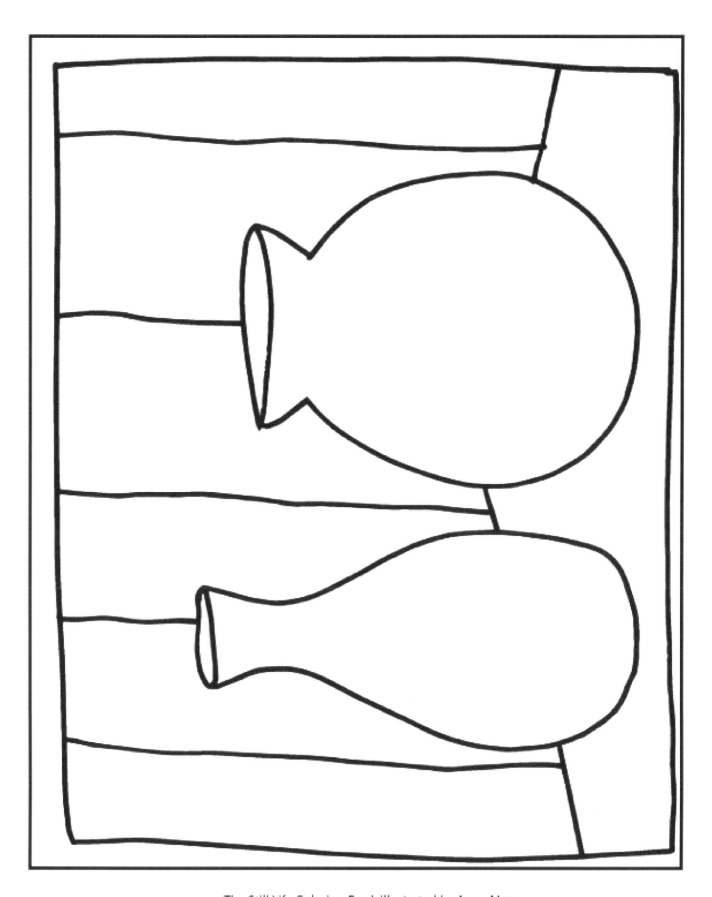

The Still Life Coloring Book illustrated by Anne Manera

The Coloring Handbook

Coloring Techniques & Step by Step Tutorials

written & illustrated by
Anne Manera

Colored Pencils Blending Coloring Page

The Coloring Handbook

Coloring Techniques & Step by Step Tutorials

written & illustrated by
Anne Manera

Colored Pencils Shading Coloring Page

Tangled Mandalas Complicated Coloring Book illustrated by Anne Manera

The Coloring Handbook

Coloring Techniques & Step by Step Tutorials

written & illustrated by
Anne Manera

Pointillism Coloring Page

The Coloring Handbook

Coloring Techniques & Step by Step Tutorials

written & illustrated by
Anne Manera

Pointillism Coloring Page

Butterfly Mandalas Coloring Book for Adults illustrated by Anne Manera

The Coloring Handbook

Coloring Techniques & Step by Step Tutorials

written & illustrated by
Anne Manera

Pointillism Coloring Page

Funky Mandalas to Tickle Your Fancy illustrated by Anne Manera

The Coloring Handbook

Coloring Techniques & Step by Step Tutorials

written & illustrated by
Anne Manera

Chalk Pastels Coloring Page

Tribal Abstract Coloring Book for All by Anne Manera

The Coloring Handbook

Coloring Techniques & Step by Step Tutorials

written & illustrated by
Anne Manera

Chalk Pastels Coloring Page

Mandala Delight Coloring Book for Adults by Anne Manera

The Coloring Handbook

Coloring Techniques & Step by Step Tutorials

written & illustrated by
Anne Manera

Impressionism Coloring Page

The Coloring Handbook

Coloring Techniques & Step by Step Tutorials

written & illustrated by
Anne Manera

Monochromatic Coloring Page

Graceful Mandalas Coloring Book & Journal illustrated by Anne Manera

The Coloring Handbook

Coloring Techniques & Step by Step Tutorials

written & illustrated by
Anne Manera

Monochromatic Coloring Page

Cat Angels Coloring Book for All illustrated by Anne Manera

The Coloring Handbook

Coloring Techniques & Step by Step Tutorials

written & illustrated by
Anne Manera

Just a #2 Pencil Coloring Page

Easy Mandalas Coloring Book for All by Anne Manera

The Coloring Handbook

Coloring Techniques & Step by Step Tutorials

written & illustrated by
Anne Manera

Just a #2 Pencil Coloring Page

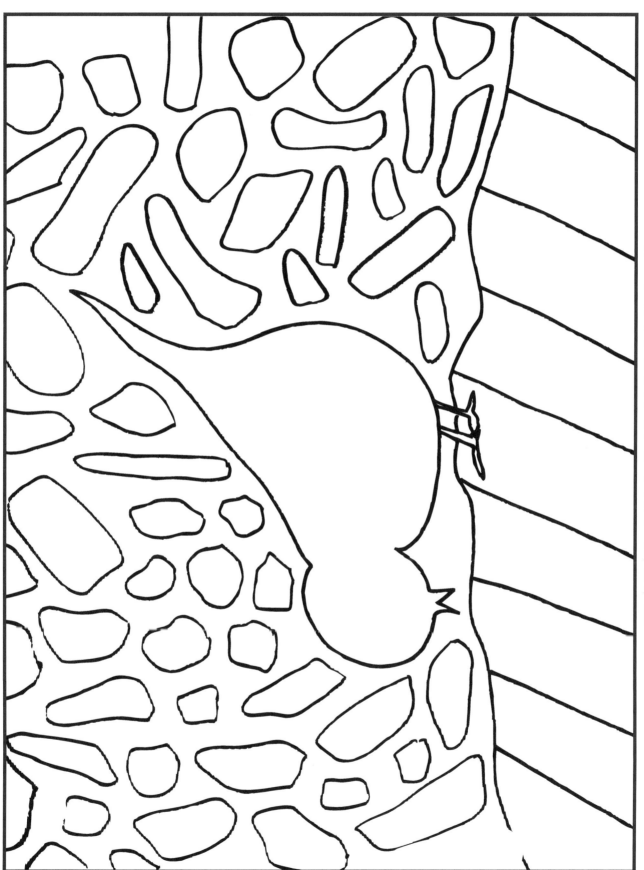

The Coloring Handbook

Coloring Techniques & Step by Step Tutorials

written & illustrated by
Anne Manera

Just a #2 Pencil Coloring Page

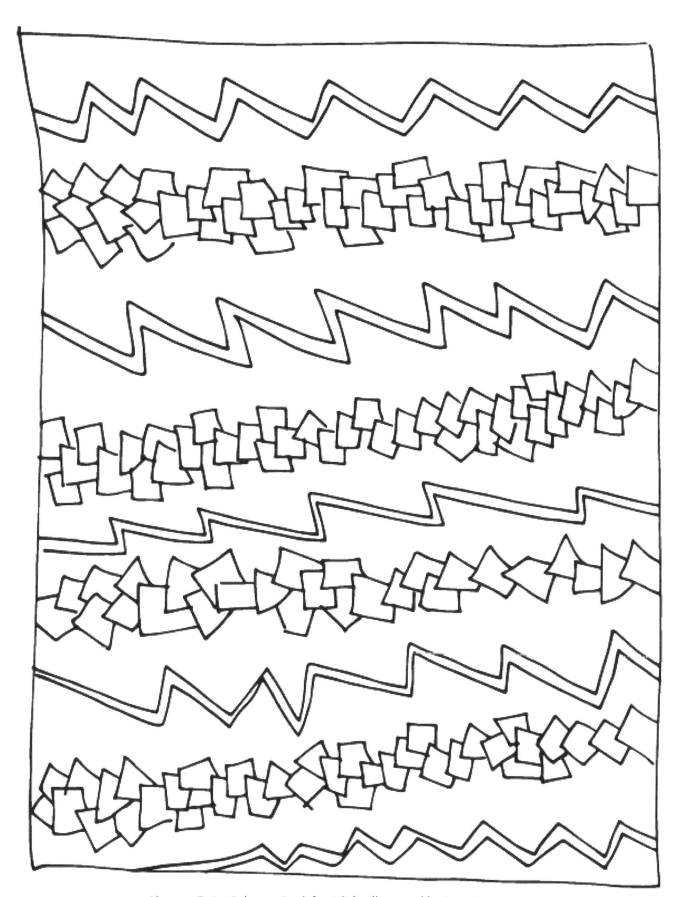

Abstract Twist Coloring Book for Adults illustrated by Anne Manera

The Coloring Handbook

Coloring Techniques & Step by Step Tutorials

written & illustrated by
Anne Manera

CPSIA information can be obtained
at www.ICGtesting.com
Printed in the USA
LVHW070138050719
623139LV00019B/715/P